My Box of Chocolates

Marvis Cox

BookLeaf Publishing

Presentation by *BookLeaf Publishing*

Web: www.bookleafpub.com

E-mail: info@bookleafpub.com

ISBN: 9789357211130

First edition 2022

ACKNOWLEDGEMENT

This book is dedicated to my beautiful wife Jacquiline, who's helped me through countless hours, days, months, and now years of life. To my mother Patricia Cox, my first love and my hero who paved the way for me and did the best she could do to raise two boys into Kings. Your hard work will always be valued and appreciated. Also to my baby brother Jeff for always keeping me grounded and reminding me to do the right thing by saying "I wouldn't do that if I was you." I heard you brother, and I get it now and I love you for just being loyal and no matter what, always staying loyal to me. My children that always keep me on my toes. My battle buddies that helped me transition from military to civilian life. My family and friends that kept pushing me to become a better person.

PREFACE

"Life is like a box of chocolates, you never know what you're gonna get."
-Forrest Gump

Drecklure PoorPay

December 1988 was a good year for me, finally got my respect, but the effect wasn't what I expected. Grandma always gave it real when it came to life. She always said you make your bed, you lay in it. Took some time before I understood what that meant. But Lord Behold that would change.

My mother worked around the clock, so she didn't have much time for us, but when we were together, it was magical. My Father could be heard coming blocks away because the tractor he drove wasn't silent at all.

The dog kept me busy, and man was it big. Sometimes aggravated from the lack of freedom. I was 7 years old once obligated to this animal, and it wasn't easy gaining its trust. Snarling, and making bashful noises as I approached carefully to gain its trust. Cunning without chase, luring me into questions without answers. But my Father's words are still in my mind. "Son, you must grab the bull by the horns, and ride the wave."

Terrified what could happen. But there's no way I would let him down. Every step was heroic, and the animal became frustrated. I can hear the growling, while steadily approaching. The smell penetrating was of piss and shit. Along with hominy all frustration. "Easy Big girl", I repeated. The basement was cold, without care. Cold drifts of air caused the hair in the back of my neck stand up. But I didn't stop going forward. I saw the shovel and broom from when someone did attempt to clean behind the animal before. Once I reached the bottom of the stairway, I heard the growl, once I grabbed the broom, I heard the bark. Then I saw the glowing, piercing eyes staring through the cracks of the wooded door. Sizing every inch of me to the core. With sounds I never heard before , and fear I never endured. Bravery was the challenge, and I had no other choice but to accept . My Faith in God wasn't present at this time, so all I had was guts. I reached down deep, and decided to open this chamber while this animal lurked. I knew I was taking a risk, but the thought of disappointing my dad seemed greater. So I opened the wooden door slowly, the dog growled deeply in a tone to let me know I'm in a combative atmosphere. This place reeks of piss and shit. And I can see it vividly at this point, but there's no way I can clean thoroughly. Unless the dog is out of the cage, what the fuck? I open the door with regret, and turn my back to walk away, while giving her space to make a decision to come out. Not sure what the out come may be , but confident in my decision. The animal sniffed its way out, locking eyes with me. Decisions were made, and we lock eyes together. The back of the animal rises, and the head lowers. I act as if I don't see it, and cautiously pursue cleaning. Inches away the animal continuously tries to engage, but I show no fear. And continue cleaning. The dog eventually moves to the opposite side of the basement. Recognizing I'm not a threat, but still on guard. While in the process of cleaning, I realize the animal laid down without worry. I didn't hear anymore snarling, or growling. So I felt comfortable for a bit, until I hade to put her back in the cage. At this point we are face to face with each other, and there is no turning back. We locked eyes, and neither of us backed down. I believe this was a test, that I could not fail. I knew this animal was much stronger, and apparently much filthier. Lol, but this was not the time for jokes. It sized me up, and I did not budge. But what I did was indifferent, and surprised me in multiple ways. I saw the animal in it's true form, and it saw me the same. And in that moment we realized we were looking in the mirror!! Giving commands to get back in the cage, but she became aggressive. She let me know fear was not an option. But once again, my father's words rang inside my head. So I spoke with a aggressive tone, back inside the cage!! She snapped at the open space, warning me of the chaos letting me know she doesn't want to go back inside the cage. Thoughts in my mind remind me failure is not an option, and this is not a choice. This is a demand, so I have to get this animal to obey my command. Terrified like my first fight, but I refuse to lose. I know if I hit her hard enough with this shovel, she will obey. But I chose to give her warning aggressively, so she can realize I mean business. She saw I wouldn't back down, and I think she understood the situation. She got her ass in that cage. That's the first time God showed me my Worth!!

Sports came easy, but my priorities needed adjustments.

It was 1988 when I first picked up a basketball. The ability to do something I was finally good at caused me to fall in love. But little did I know, I had a lot of work to do, before anyone would see me as a good player. Up and down the gym, running suicides all evening would be the punishment if you missed a shot. My coach was young, and still immature to the game. But he made up with his ruthless conditioning drills. Sometimes the team would question his authority, but we paid for it with sweat, and tears after the fact. Everybody swore they were the best players on the team. It took some time to actually start working together. Everybody had something that would single them out. My gift was speed. Nobody on the team could run faster than me. But I lacked fundamentals. Knowing how to get down the court the fastest was one thing, but making the basket was another. Plus I only used my right hand for everything, which made me predictable. My shooting abilities weren't the greatest , but I made up with a relentless will to win. Coach stayed on my neck about poor decision making, and using my left hand more. So I spent my summer break working on my form, and using my left hand more. Most of the times, I would stay up all night, until the next day, working on these skills. It would be so early in the morning, and everybody on the block was sleep. I was the only one awake, working towards my goal. That's when I started to notice a strange, calming, peace. It felt as if I was the only person in the world, and I had the whole world all to myself. So my focus was on point, without interruptions. I was nervous about Basketball Camp, because I feared my teammates would make fun of me again. Even with all the hard work I put myself through, my confidence was questioned. Our first game was on a rainy day, this will be my opportunity to show off my skills,or soI thought But the coach didn't put me in the game. I ask him many times, why can't I go in coach? And he replied I wasn't ready. Three days go by, and still no game play. The last day of camp, one of the guys were fouled really hard, and had to sit out. We didn't have all our players that day, so coach had no other choice but to allow me in the game. We were victorious, and the coach was jumping, and clapping his hands like a crazy person. He couldn't believe I was the same person who couldn't make a basket, and made poor decisions. The little time I played, I scored twelve points with minutes left on the clock. Even my teammates were over joyed with my improvements. They cheered me on as the game ended. From that point on, I was finally labeled as a Basketball Player. Because we won the entire competition, we were allowed to go swimming. Everyone was excited to swim, but once again, I was nervous as shit. I love the water, but I'm deeply terrified of deep water. Plus I didn't know how to swim, so here we go again, doing something I know needed improvement. I didn't tell anyone I lacked the skill to swim, so I stayed in the shallow end. We were having a ball, but then my teammates started going deeper, and deeper in the pool. Regardless of my fear of water, I wouldn't allow that to determine my participation. I hung on close to the side of the pool, and followed the rest of the group. I figured as long as I have something to hang on with, I should be good. But some of the team was in one part of the pool, where it drops off to the deep end. I didn't realize this before I decided to play with them as well. I bounced up and down in the area to reassure my confidence. But the waves were pushing me further into the deep end. Then all of a sudden I felt nothing under my feet. And that's when the panic started to kick in. I tried, and tried to resurface to the top. But my body never fully came all the way up. Once I started to choke, I swallowed a large amount of water. And my lungs were filled with water almost instantly. My body started to drift in, and out of consciousnesses. I knew I was dying, and I was so afraid. Eventually all my movements stoped, and I saw this black dot in the center of my blurred vision. And the dot expanded to a wider darkness, as I slowly fade away. I can see my teammates playing in the water above me. I'm trying my best to hold on to the voice in my head screaming help, but no one can hear me. Everything goes black, and I'm gone!!!

Tread Lightly

Then suddenly I open my eyes barely, feeling my hand clutching to someone's foot. Once my hand felt something, I guess my nerves reacted and grabbed whatever it was. Luckily it was one of my teammates, and he couldn't shake me off. So they worked as a team to pull me out of the water. Once I was brought to the surface I immediately started to regurgitate all the fluids consumed. My teammates worked together, and swam me to the shallow end of the pool. I couldn't stop coughing, and with every cough my head felt like it would explode. I stayed in that one spot for at least an hour thinking, I just died, and came back to life, wow!! My eyes were blood shot red, and I had a headache out of this world. When I shook my head, I could feel water inside my brain. If it wasn't water inside my brain, it sure felt like it. This headache and water on the brain lasted for three days nonstop. Finally I started to feel better, and that's when it hit me. All that time I spent trying to master Basketball, I should have spent learning how to swim.

My dad always said there was no such thing as friends!!

Moving to new areas always bring controversy as a child. As soon as my mother let me and my brother outside, these ugly ass dudes down the street start mugging us. I had a lot of fights that summer, creeps always wanna to try the new guys. Me and my brother eventually met a set cool of peoples once it started to get cold outside. That's when we would play football. We love to play football in the snow, or any bad weather. It made us feel like we were super stars on T.V. Back in the days football was the sport to play. Everybody wanted to be a football player, and no matter how good, or bad things were at home. We left all our frustration, and anger on the field. The aggressiveness, and violence of the sport seemed like art to me. So every time I got the chance, I wanted to be (Picasso). Playing sports always bring people together. So I made some friends finally. Me and the guys would link up and play either sports, or video games. If we didn't play either of those, we would play a game called Porch Hopping. Porch Hopping consisted of running as fast as you can, and jumping to the ledge of an apartment, or house near each other. When I was growing up they use to call me the Dare Devil. Because I would always take things to the another level, or the extreme. I would be lying if I told you I wasn't addicted to adrenaline. One day some of my buddies found a way to get on top of their two story apartment building. The feeling of being so high in the sky made me afraid, but feel so alive at the same time. Looking over the edge gave me a vision how high we was from the ground. That's when I noticed the space between buildings, and came up with a crazy idea. Hey y'all bet I can jump from this building to the other!

Had to be the longest 15 minute drive of my life.

While laying in the bed with her, my mind couldn't help but wonder? Is this the last time I would be alive. No need for sex, it was time to just lay. While enjoying each other's company, the night drew us closer. As I layer there, feeling the tears fall on my chest. All I could do was be quiet, the room stood still, and the air felt thick. Unsure how to break the ice, but I felt greatly this was the last time we would spend together. After a couple hours thinking relentlessly, my phone rang. It was Drexture, one of my soldiers trying to build his courage to do the unforgiving. He reassured his readiness for War, but his heart seemed heavy. I tried to uplift his confidence, but wasn't sure if it went over his head. My alarm went off aggressively, and that's when reality set in. An eerie feeling surfaced the air, I looked outside, and all I saw was fog. Fuck, it's time to go. My bags were packed, I even doubled checked to make sure nothing was missing. I was lacing my boots when I noticed she became distant. She was in need of emotional support, so she called her mother to ride along with us to the Military Base. I did a double check, to get one last glace of the place I called a home behind. I saw a bottle of Grey Goose on the counter given to me for my birthday, and decided to take one last shot. Damn, that hit the spot!! Normally I would drive, but this time I decided to ride in the back seat. This was a good time to reflect on what's about to occur, and that's when it finally hit me, I'm going to War.

Here it is me, and some fellow soldiers sitting in a hummer armored vehicle. 12 hour shift was almost done.

Prayers rang over multiple Speakers though out the city every morning. Me, Beckum, and Rally was on guard this particular morning. I was on the machine Gun, Beckum was the driver, and Rally was manning the radio. Unlike any day, we took note of our surroundings, while joking with each other at the same time. The radio was full of commotion, because one of our teams got hit by a land mine in the area. Thank God, nobody was hurt. In this country I've seen so many sun rises, and so many sun sets. This morning we were graced with a beautiful sunrise, that spread all over the valley. We were one of six Armored vehicles surrounding our compound. Which happened to be an old twelve story building rittled with bullet holes, and bomb fragments. I noticed from a far, our guard relief was approaching. I didn't understand, because I still had two hours left before our shift was over with. I also noticed my Commander was with them, which caused me to be very nervous. My Commander called for me to come down from the machine gun with worry in his eyes. Then that's when he told me, my Grandmother has passed away. He gave instructions for me to return tobase, and prepare to go home.

What did I do to make things so complicated?

Being a child was a memory that I can't remember much of, just small glimpse of the pass circumventing. I still try to remember what my favorite toy was. I remember my brothers favorite toy was a teddy bear named Teddy Rubskin. Teddy sang all types of great songs, even moved along to the beat while singing. What freaked me out about Teddy, was that his eyes, and mouth moved like a real bear. So at times when Teddy told stories, it's eyes would make contact, and leave an eerie feeling. I didn't feel safe around Teddy, but my brother loved him. One night I woke to a mysterious noise in the kitchen. I went to investigate quietly, and what I saw can't be explained. Goosebumps sent chills down my spine, as I watched Teddy eating leftover chicken mom made the night before. Teddy wasn't just eating the chicken, it was devouring the chicken. I was stricken with fear, and shock has taken over my body. Finally I built up the confidence to walk away from what I've just witnessed. But inside the apartment complex, we had old wood floors. And if not careful, the creaking sounds could wake the entire place. Well just my luck, I stepped back onto the floor causing a low toned creaking sound. That seemed to drag on the more I applied my weight. The sound caught me by surprise, so I looked back quickly to see what it was. How could I have done this foolish mistake, pondered my mind? Immediately I felt great discomfort, because if I heard this noise? Then I know Teddy did as well. While turning my head towards the kitchen, I caught a shadow approaching me slowly. At this point I'm drenched in cold sweat, unsure what terror I'm about to face. Out the darkness of the kitchen my brother walks, rubbing his eyes, asking what I'm doing up so late? I let a sigh out in relief it was my brother, and not Teddy. I didn't want to freak him out, so I only asked where Teddy was? And never mentioned what I saw. As we were walking back to his room, he explained that Teddy was in the bed with him the whole night. When I cut the lights on, there it was, Teddy Rubskin. No food around its mouth, no smell of food. I was confused, so I asked my brother, was you in the kitchen eating the leftover chicken? He said no, just woke up cause I heard a noise coming from the kitchen. All of a sudden, complete darkness. We both jumped in fear because the lights went out, once I looked towards the bed, Teddy wasn't there.

Lil boy you are covered

Shook away the covers, phone ringing off the hook, looking for my brother, but he's no were I can look. What have I've discovered, by myself, no one left. Pistol in my hand, three bullets, and war I declare. Kinda figured it was nation business, my father told me ain't no such thing as friends, so you know I'm relentless. Four hundred grand used as a pillow, and my head still hurt. Lost a lot family members, but my legs still work. Born to die, living the city of the Chi. Giving my all, through trails and tribulations Covid 19 got me masked up, like I'm Jason.

Friends

Friendships didn't last
Ever since I lost my cash
I remember when I had thousands
I was stuntin on they ass!!!
Riding around the hood bouncing
Trying not to scrape the curve
Fam hit me on the phone,
I'm like "Joe what's the word??"
People love to scream peace when they get their ass disturbed, I like to fuckin eat in peace
While I'm smoking on this herb,
Deep internal thoughts
About all the shit in life ta be the boss,
In the back of my mind I know there's a cost,
So when the reaper come running
I get ta dumping,
Funny feelings in my stomach
Like I'm born to do something
But what!
It's like I'm left with questions I can't answer
Promise to never live on my knees
So u kno ya boy stands up!!!
Lord help me!!!!
Is what I recommend
I can't perpetrate to be something less than ah man

Devastating battles in life
As I comprehend my daddy told me “Ain’t no such thing as no motherfuckin friend!!!”

Destiny

These goofies talk bout taking lives
Ain't lived theirs yet!
But I be talking about taking wives and rolling in jets!!
Man I'm hip to the game
That's why they call me a vet,
And I been known to take lives
I just ain't took yours yet!!!
No need to give me cash dawg
Man just cut me a check!

Not into relationship
That shit is a hassle,
More into dealerships
And counting my cash flow
Man I got a choke on life
While grabbing the wind pipe,
Dipping in and out of lanes
Getting brain from somebody's wife
I don't know what your life is like
But mine is real like getting searched by the cops
And you hiding that steel,
Whole mouth full of dope while trying my best not to swallow!
Living fast in the day just to see tomorrow

Body full of scars and my heart is hollow
Praying to God with sweaty palms
Cause these dicks searching my Tahoe!
Was supposed to pick shorty up
Guess I'm gonna be late,
Visualizing disappointment on my daughters face
Staring at me in ah cage
Heart pumping and full of rage!!
Why me?
Street life got a hold of my destiny

Brother Marvin

As a youngster I had a big heart
Til I was burned in the dark
Lil brother was bigger than me
So my times were even harder
Moms taught me how to punch,
Cause it wasn't no Father,
He was gone so I was on my own
Put a mattress on the wall
Beat it until I got strong
So when it came to brawling dog,
You know it was on,
Dope Boyz influenced me
Riding around in their chevys
Look in the windows
Can't see cause they smoking real heavy
Everytime tha chicks see em
They all be going crazy
That's when I knew that my time was gone come
Yeah man!!!!
My Boy Big Trav introduced me to guns,
Love at first sight so you know I got one!
Empty shell in tha 38 is what my folks didn't
know,
Pull tha trigger on them dudes
Watch they ass hit the floe
If u dare me mother fucka show u how I act up

Everybody in the streets knew I didn't give a fuck
I don't know about Usher
But I got it bad
Money started coming in so I got a bag!!
All at the mall dog with my pants at a sag!
Ten guys with me leaving the mall like we carrying out the trash,
All for the love of the dough,
3 things in life guaranteed,
Taxes,
Death, and
Trouble
Like Marvin Gaye said "I came up HARD"

Unforgettable Steps, Unforgiving Ways

Chances taken to see how much life is, compared to knowing if Love was. Born while my father denies ties with his child because his/her skin is lighter than others" wishing to take back words are no longer an option. Much hope with plenty denial is what I call my childhood. So much movement you would think we were machines.. Everybody has a task to perform, but I'm slow at perfecting mines. Heart big as the universe, but everybody doesn't feel the same. I feel alone, and scared, while others feel the same. Am I repeating myself? Am I denying unfairness while trying to play the cards I was dealt?

The Transition

Friendships didn't last
Ever since I lost my cash
I remember when I had thousands
I was stuntin on they ass!!!
Riding around the hood bouncing
Trying not to scrape the curve
Fam hit me on the phone,
I'm like "Bro what's the word??"
People love to scream peace when they get their ass disturbed, I like to fuckin eat in peace
While I'm smoking on this herb,
Deep internal thoughts
About all the shit I did In life ta be the boss,
In back of my mind I know there's a cost,
So when the reaper come running
I get ta dumping,
Funny feelings in my stomach
Like I'm born to do something
But what!
It's like I'm left with questions I can't answer
Promise to never live on my knees
So u kno tha boy stands up!!!
Lord help me!!!!
Is what I recommend
I can't perpetrate to be something less then ah man

Devastating battles in life
As I comprehend my daddy told me “Ain’t no such thing as no fuckin friend!!!”

Summer Nights

Summer Nights Never Seemed The Same Again

Watching T.V with my brother, drinking Kool Aid was normal for me. We use to take bread and dip it in the Kool Aid. That was such a treat. It didn't take much to please us, we were content with what we had. My mother, and father were in the master bedroom that particular night. What made me remember was the door being shut, and loud commotion carrying on. I didn't think anything of it, until the argument started to spill where me and my brother was located. Inside of our apartment, the hallways were long. I use to visualize being in a train station, every time I walked down the halls. The light inside of the room my mother was in seemed to be extremely bright. This would make the shadow of my father huge coming down the hallway. I can't recall all the things my mother was saying, but it was extremely loud. Me and my brother covered our ears, but it didn't drain out the sound. My father shadow appeared huge on the walls, but grew smaller as he got closer. His words kept echoing in the hall. So That's It Then, I'm Leaving! Me and my brother stood in awe, confused as to what washappening. I ran to my mother to console her, but she kept crying profusely. I let her know that night she would never have to worry, because I won't leave her side. And one day I would have so much money to buy her a house, and anything else she wanted. She slowly looked up, and smiled saying don't worry about mommy. Little did she know, that made me worry even more.

Nu Nu Day

It's ah new day
Funny how my scares start to itch
Staring at the mirror seeing old age without growth
Ain't life ah bitch?
I know I'm praying on a daily basis
While life is steady laughing at me
Remembering things is ah blurr
Starting to remind me of my pappy
How can things become ah distance
When it was just at arms reach

She say she love me for who I am But cold at the heart
The hunt in the sea Blue orchard chasing the shark
Even in the dark these types of things should never spark
All I needed was her answers
And I will give questions
When I was with my step father
The police seem to rush in
The anger started rush in But I had to calm my thoughts

My cousin griped my hand real tight before his life was lost
Split second of living real life is what these people cost
But I'm supposed to suppress my anger
In the clutch of total strangers
If I had ah gun I would have won
Because I would have been quicker and faster
Never to allow the repeatitions of such disasters

Denzel to the Bull

Feels like I'm getting stronger, world upon my shoulders, destiny and faith, we all set a date pushing hard to get this money, trying to get this profit in, flying upside down, Denzel Washingtin appointments set, Yep, I know I'm next, Yep! Moving through the intersection like ah T Rex, just to hide the connect, Nas playing on the radio, all I need is one mic" Glock 40ty just in case they get on me, all I need is one site, Boom!! Suit case of assumption to be the man, while dodging the bullet to beat the can, ain't no way they gone stop my legacy, to take me out, it's gone take more then word of mouth muthaf*****, being ah sucka, not me, being a pussy, not me, I suffered to much, I know what it's like to bleed. Family was my go to, now all I see is Enemies, Fuck No I'm not like you, I am a different Breed, we may have came from the same tree but, ain't shit shaking but the Leaves! When pressure builds, the pipes bust, I witnessed so many love ones put in dirt, my pappy dead and mother still alive, but I still feel the hurt

Boy II Man

At an early age my childhood was snatched from me. Once my father left us, things started to go down hill. My mother had to work so much, that it left me and my brother fending for ourselves. Unfair, and unjust showed itself sooner then I expected. Seeing how life has become for me, and my family since my father left made me loose respect for men. I felt men were weak, and women were strong. Illusions of the mind will take its toll after living in fear how a child can protect it's family, and what's on the menu to eat the next day. My mother worked sixteen hour shift everyday just to keep us afloat. Responsibilities became over bearing, so me and my brother had to move on with my grandmother. I remember the first day my mother dropped us off at our grandmas house. My grandma seemed so caring, but stern. It was hard to figure out which one she was. The move was rushed, because my mother hade to be at work in a couple hours. I didn't feel comfortable, and wanted to leave with my mother. But she told me to stay strong, and help look after my brother. She handed me my favorite toy, gave me a hug, and left out the door. I immediately felt defeated, and all alone.

My grandmother came rushing to me, and took my toy away.

While leading me by the arm to the kitchen table. Wham, a book came crashing on the table with force. There's no time to play anymore, read this if you want entertainment. I looked closer, and saw it was a Encyclopedia. I knew things were not the same, and life for me, and my brother would become very different.

Inside the Mind of a MAINE MAN

All that shit I did to not be like my father went out the fucking window.... maybe somewhere somehow he's always been in my heart and I've always been his shadow.... people fear what they don't understand. Raised by women maybe my fear was how to become a REAL MAN.... now I see... now I know. I'm in control, and I am secure in it. I thank God for it.

Son

If I ask you a question you don't know
You don't know
Every time I make conversation you don't know
You don't know
20 years and you about to be 21 yo
21 bro
Shit get old when you say that you don't know
You don't know!!
I'm steady speaking when not spoken to
You know how I do
Trying to understand what's to you
Wearing different shoes
What the fuck happen to us bra?
I gave you so much love
Now you tell me you have no passion
No trust
I extend my hand to show compassion and love
But it's all good
I couldn't change you
And if I could
I'll let you know we from different hoods
Misunderstood
But you can't cry over spilled milk
When the earth always drinks from guilt
And Blood show no love
You better ask about me cuz!

I'm ah different breed
Like Crack
Give them what they need
Blood pumping in my shoulders
Wearing my heart on my sleeves
I thought if I get older I would change how I be
But the more I get older
I always change out my sheets
It's always challenging to me to understand what's going on
Christmas and New Years Eve always seemed to be going wrong
I tried to be a farther, but that's not what Your people wanted. I guess they wished for me to walk around with my head down, and a weak stomach.
But tell them not him, not me. Like I said before I am a different breed. And one day when your old enough, and the other half of your DNA take control of stuff. You will be a different breed too.

Real Life Dreams

Dream

About going on a vacation, was supposed to be free. Me, a young boy, and couple male friends. The place seemed like a huge theme park, but things took a turn once we as a group started looking for our rooms. One of our friends took the elevator to get to their room no problem. But the rest of us had rooms on the other side of the park. Once we got to our area, we hopped on an elevator. But the elevator took took us around the park, but never up to our rooms. That's when we noticed things were not what they seemed. We got off the elevators, to use the bathroom. And come to find out, it wasn't free to use the restroom. Then we tried to get water, and it also wasn't free. Things started to get really weird once we saw all these people in this section of the park doing drugs, or what they thought were drugs. Happiness turned into fear because we knew we had a small amount of money.

Prodigal Son

I don’t apologize for nothing
Never will they catch me slipping
Without clutching my gun
Close to understanding life
Like the moon and the Sun
Face my enemies, by any means
I’m the Prodigal Son

Im steady call her, she stay giving shade
Back an forward from chi nights
To California days
Knowing her folks threatened me
I still come through like summer breeze
An the tease of my daughter being close to me
Couldn’t imagine this young girl so close to me
Finally meet her, now she screaming she wants to leave
These situations seems so gross to me
I stuck my hand out, she starts to wild out
Her aunt steady telling me this ain’t the time now
I’m so confused man, so confused man!!
Came all the way from Chicago, confused man
Pushed my way to California, like I was kicking cans, I know you hate me, but I’m ah different man

I gave all that was dealt, when it came to playing my cards, this all that was left
You say you hate me, I get it.
But it's trials and tribulations, from ones that guilty, and who did it. I failed at times between you and I, I must admit your dad was the shit.
Pushed start the car to a foreign whip
To my wife now, I'm alright now!!
She telling me it's ok, but I prayed it would never be this way
I don't apologize for None!!

www.ingramcontent.com/pod-product-compliance
Lightning Source LLC
Chambersburg PA
CBHW051742130826
49812CB00033B/966
* 9 7 8 9 3 5 7 2 1 1 1 3 0 *